Second Sight

~ Also by George Held ~

Under the Escalator
New York, NY: Filsinger and Company, 2018

Dog Hill Poems
Seattle, WA: Goldfish Press, 2017

Phased II
Hoboken, NJ: Poets Wear Prada, 2016

Bleak Splendor
Brookline, MA: Muddy River Books, 2015

Neighbors: The Water Critters
illustrated by Joung Un Kim
New York, NY: Filsinger and Company, 2015

Culling: New & Selected Nature Poems
Hoboken, NJ: Poets Wear Prada, 2014

Neighbors: The Yard Critters Too
illustrated by Joung Un Kim
New York, NY: Filsinger and Company, 2013

Neighbors: The Yard Critters, Book 1
illustrated by Joung Un Kim
New York, NY: Filsinger and Company, 2011

After Shakespeare: Selected Sonnets
W. Somerville, MA: Červená Barva Press, 2011

Phased
Hoboken, NJ: Poets Wear Prada, 2008

The News Today
W. Somerville, MA: Červená Barva Press, 2008

The Art of Writing and Others
Georgetown, KY: Finishing Line Press, 2007

W Is for War
W. Somerville, MA: Červená Barva Press, 2006

Martial Artist, translator
Claremont, CA: Toad Press, 2005

Grounded
Georgetown, KY: Finishing Line Press, 2005

Untitled e-book
Nashville, TN: *The HyperTexts*, 2004

American Poetry
Farrell, PA: New Formalist Press, 2003

Touched by Eros, editor
Islip, NY: The Live Poets Society, 2002

Beyond Renewal
Mena, AR: Cedar Hill Publications, 2001

Absolut Death and Others
with paintings by Roz Dimon
New York, NY: Dimon Studios, 2000

Open and Shut: Cinquains
Talent, OR: Talent House Press, 1999

Salamander Love and Others
Talent, OR: Talent House Press, 1998

Winged
Northport, NY: Birnham Wood Graphics, 1995

Second Sight
Poems

GEORGE HELD

POETS WEAR PRADA • Hoboken, New Jersey

Second Sight

Copyright © 2019 George Held

All rights reserved. Except for use in any review or for educational purposes, the reproduction or utilization of this work in whole or in part in any form by electronic, mechanical or other means, now known or hereafter invented, including xerography, photocopying and recording, or in any informational or retrieval system, is forbidden without the written permission of the publisher:

>Poets Wear Prada
>533 Bloomfield Street, Second Floor
>Hoboken, New Jersey 07030
>http://pwpbooks.blogspot.com

First North American Publication 2019
First Mass Market Paperback Edition 2019

Grateful acknowledgment is made to the following publications, where some of these poems first appeared:

>*Blue Unicorn, Casserole, The Deronda Review, First Literary Review — East, Five Willows Literary Review, HitchLit Review, Home Planet News Online, Literary Matters, Negative Capability, Ol' Chanty, Peacock Journal, Plainsongs, String Poet, Under a Warm Green Linden,* and *Xanadu.*

ISBN-13: 978-1-946116-02-4   ISBN-10: 1-946116-02-5

Printed in the U.S.A.

Front Cover Design: Roxanne Hoffman
Author Photo: Cheryl Filsinger

For Cheryl

Table of Contents

Laura Bridgman and the Mouse	3
Celestial	5
Give Me Shelter (Yggdrasil's Legacy)	7
Hyacinths for My Love	9
Why I Never Go to Church Anymore	10
Sunday Morning	13
Tamar's Lament	15
Onan	16
Eostre / Ēostre	17
Cædmon among the Cows	18
Fragment	19
Desire	20
Like Cavafy	21
A Bearded Old Poet	22
Acid Peace	23
Answering the Call	25
Rats!	26
Kite Flying	27
Acknowledgments	28
About the Author	29

Second Sight

Laura Bridgman and the Mouse

I wad be laith to rin an' chase thee
Wi' murd'ring pattle.
        — Robert Burns, "To a Mouse"

In the confines of her chamber
at Perkins, Laura daydreams
of flying out the window —
then she senses the brush
of fur along the baseboard.

"O it's that mouse again," she
exclaims, growing furious
to think of its temerity
invading her familiar space
like some nether Sam Howe

before he met Julia Ward
and lost interest in Laura.
"O that dratted mouse," she
says and spontaneously
turns predatory.

Her acute feeling, like a bat's
echolocation, homes in
on that "wee sleekit cowran
tim'rous beastie" spared
by Mr. Burns's tolerance.

Miss Bridgman, with her best
square-dancing form, takes steps
left and right, forward but rarely
back, tracking the mouse

into a corner where it cowers.

The second sight of the blind
empowers the young woman
to spring, with one shoe forward,
upon the mouse and start stomping
the stuffing out of him, and how!

Laura Dewey Lynn Bridgman (1829 – 1889), the first deaf-blind child to be educated in America — fifty years in advance of the more celebrated Helen Keller — learned to read and write at the Perkins School for the Blind in Boston, under the direction of Dr. Samuel Gridley Howe. Laura came to the school just prior to her eighth birthday, living there with Dr. Howe and his sister from 1837 until his marriage to Julia Ward in 1843. Howe, Laura's legal guardian, primary educator, and once devoted champion, continued to provide for her financially, but, according to biographers, his interests were not unaffected by marriage. His wife, who gave birth to their first child while the couple was enjoying an extended honeymoon in Europe, had career ambitions of her own and did not share Howe's interest in the blind. Laura remained at the school as a full-time resident and part-time teacher, eventually meeting and sharing a cottage on the campus with Anne Sullivan in the 1880s. Laura outlived Howe, who died in 1876.

Celestial

When I was a kid, one winter's night
my Uncle Mike drew me out to the lawn
and pointed at the sky. "That's Officer
O'Ryan up there. See his nightstick
held high and his belt with pistol?"

When Sister Margaret, the astronomer,
lover of the night sky, pointed at her
celestial chart and asked us to identify
that same cluster of stars, "a con-stel-
la-tion, a gathering of stars," she said,

my hand shot up, and called upon,
I said, "That's Officer O'Ryan, patrolling
the night skies," and Stella O'Reilly,
my great crush, tittered while Sister
Margaret rolled her eyes, then gladly

began to tell us the stellar history
of Orion the Hunter, identified so by
the Greeks, envisioned as holding
a club, not a nightstick, and wearing
a sword, not a gun, in his belt,

and pointed to its two great stars,
Betelgeuse and Rigel, seventh brightest
in our universe and "luminous
as the sun," I held back tears
until I saw the humor in it —

Uncle Mike pulling my leg, my desire
to shine like the sun for Sister Margaret

and Stella O'Reilly, only to be eclipsed
by my eager false answer, and the giant
constellation, since known as O'Rion.

Give Me Shelter (Yggdrasil's Legacy)
For Lars Espeland

Central to Norse mythology
stands Yggdrasil, the giant ash tree,
in whose name are traces
of "gallows" — Odin hanged himself
from it — and "terror": to the tune
of "O Tannenbaum," sing we,
"O terror tree, O terror tree . . ."

As a kid I loved a tall white pine
against whom I'd press my spine
when doom hung over me;
when I read of Yggdrasil
I dreamed of trying to hug him,
an impossibility, for no arms
could encircle that huge trunk.

What better to dispel gloom
than to embrace terror, to hug
an immense tree, even if its resin
stained my tee and made Mom
angry at me. The pine smelled
forest fresh, but how would
Yggdrasil smell, like mountain ash?

O terror tree, O terror tree,
please take pity on puny me,
be my tree of life, root me
as you are rooted to three
wellsprings while your limbs
reach into the heavens and shelter
dragon, eagle, and stag.

Leave me earth locked like thee,
heaven bound for eternity.

Hyacinths for My Love

> You gave me hyacinths first a year ago;
> They called me the hyacinth girl.
> — T.S. Eliot, "The Waste Land"

Greek Hyacinth is twice lamented —
first, struck dead by Apollo's discus
and now superseded by Eliot's girl.

How romantic to be called
"the hyacinth girl," singled out by a gift
of strong-scented flowers that left me faint.

Apollo's memorial hyacinth was red
for the blood of discus-killed Hyacinth
but today is as likely blue or white,

the color of innocence. Innocent
were both Hyacinth and the hyacinth girl,
caught in the immortal nexus

of "The Waste Land." They give
it color. And to think that you fancied
yourself "the hyacinth girl"

in your fey romanticism: you
wanted from me for birthday and Easter
blue hyacinths to symbolize our love,

and I gave you them as short as love
did last, until you vanished with Edgar
and left me holding wilted flowers.

Why I Never Go to Church Anymore

I never go to church anymore
though I went every Sunday
when I was a boy.

I liked my simple church,
the Greenville Community Church,
a Dutch Reformed church.

It was built in 1842 on a hillside
along a major road, now Route 100,
and its cemetery sat beside

and behind the church
and its assembly hall, where
Youth Fellowship met

on Sunday evenings.
My mom was the soprano
soloist in the church choir,

and was much admired
for her soaring voice that
reached all the way to God,

though the choir loft was actually
at ground level next to the pulpit,
where the Reverend Theodore

(beloved of God) Brinckerhoff
preached the word of God
every Sunday at 11 AM.

He preached that Jesus

was the son of God and might
have been of virgin birth,

but Mary was just a young mother,
not anyone to pray to (like
the Catholics), and Jesus

might, after crucifixion,
have been resurrected,
but it was up to each and every

one of us to decide these things
for ourselves. I figured the Rev.
Mr. Brinckerhoff didn't cotton

to the supernatural
readings of the Lord's life,
and I took the slacker's way

and shrugged them off. I liked
Jesus okay as just the son of God:
that was enough for me

until I went to college and read
Niebuhr, Barth, Kierkegaard,
who had a hard time with dogma

and tried to conjure a faith
relevant to modern times,
and I let them lead me astray

so I dropped out of the Church
team at my fraternity, a few guys
who went to church with hang-

overs every Sunday, and in the

chill morning sun of Providence,
Rhode Island, I thought hard

about the Baby Jesus, and the
rabble-rousing Jesus, and the
poor beat Jesus hanging

on a cross at thirty-three and dying
wretchedly of exposure
and shock with other criminals

at Golgotha, until it didn't
matter anymore, God didn't
matter anymore, and I was

consigned to a life unmonitored
by God, and that's why
I never go to church anymore.

Sunday Morning
Pantoum

We meet every Sunday morning,
Parishioners long apostate
From any established church,
To worship at the font of Venus.

Parishioners long apostate,
We thirst for vital ritual
To worship at the font of Venus
And slake our thirst through thrust.

We thirst for vital ritual
Through our bodies, not our souls,
And slake our thirst through thrust
And parry, passion and control

Of our bodies, not our souls.
We doff our Sunday garb and naked
We parry passion and control
Like sun worshipers or cannibals.

We doff our Sunday garb, get naked
And tear at life down to the bone,
As sun worshipers or cannibals
Feed a hunger deep in the gut

And tear at life down to the bone,
Leave no morsel on the altar,
Feeding hunger deep in the gut,
Sparing not self or the other.

Leaving no morsel on the altar
Of any established church,

Sparing not self or the other,
We meet every Sunday morning.

Tamar's Lament

> He spilled it on the ground, lest that he should give seed to his brother.
> — Genesis 38.9

After the Lord had slain my husband,
his father told Onan, his surviving son,
to do his duty, to service me, Tamar,
provide his seed in Er's stead.

Onan was on the spot — I had ever
felt his heat, but he feared
I might be the one who made Er sinful
in the sight of the Lord.

When Onan came to me, he found me
receptive, even eager, so long
had I lain alone a widow.
I made room for him on the pallet

and uncovered myself. Aroused,
he nevertheless hesitated as I
longed for him to kneel and enter me.
But "No!" he said, adamant in refusal

to give seed for his brother; though I
clasped his arm, he pulled himself
out of my hold and stepped back,
stroking himself until, quite speedily,

he spilled his seed onto the ground.
I groaned watching him waste our progeny,
then step outside, only to be struck down
by the wrath of the Lord.

Onan
After Genesis 38.9

For "spilling my seed" my name has become
opprobrious: *onanism*, the euphemism
for masturbation — as if I'd merely
gratified myself. The rabbis, at least,

condemned me only for failing to procreate.
It was the Enlightenment that cast
a scientific eye upon my deed, that
made it deplorable to ease oneself.

Who cared that spilling seed denied
a chance for life in a world already
thick with brats? The issue wasn't issue
but that anyone might please oneself,

might prefer solitude and the power
of the imagination to create
more delicious images of desire
than real bodies could flesh out,

might know better than anyone else
the speed and pressure of the stroke
to maximize the, ah, pleasure,
with no unwelcome outcome.

Eostre / Ēostre

You, my lady, are the feminine side
of the Christ, though you are pagan
and He founded the Christian Church.

As a woman, you contain myriad eggs,
and legend says, one winter's day,
you revived a bird with frozen wings

by, Circe-like, turning it into a rabbit,
a mammal known for fecundity,
and yet, you carried over the bird's

ability to lay eggs: the curious
now extinct oviparous rabbit then
turned into the Easter Bunny, and so,

on that floating, moon-measured holiday
called by your name, we recall
the resurrection of a frozen bird

and the Resurrection of the Word.

Cædmon among the Cows

Drunk on mead, England's first
Poet-to-be left the great hall
And fell asleep

Among cows in the barn.
In a dream "Cædmon's Hymn"
Came to him:

"Nu scylun hergan," it
Begins: "Now we shall praise
The Guardian of heaven . . ."

Mead, dream, poem:
Cædmon chosen
While cows chew their cud.

Second half-line, "hefaenrices uard," omitted here, translates to "the Guardian of heaven." Early Northumbrian "Moore" version (CUL MS Kk 5.16, c. 737)

Fragment

the Spanish festival of Transhumance,
celebrated since the days of Romance,
when shepherds and sheep shall dance
over the Pyrenees and into France

Desire

In Burne-Jones's pencil drawing *Desiderium*,
the androgynous image of his Greek lover,
Maria, in profile, appears flushed, aroused,
her long neck a Pre-Raphaelite emblem.

In the Tate, the figure's half-closed eyes seem
fixed on an unseen object of desire,
the sensuous full lips parted to admit it.

Only Hollyer's photo of the whole piece,
before it was trimmed to the right of her face,
shows, faintly, her hand cupping a scrotum,
above which extends, almost touching her face,
the glans and shaft of an erect penis.

Like Cavafy

Like Cavafy, I first wrote sonnets,
Then found a freer form of verse.
Like Cavafy, I cherish my digs, not
Above a brothel, but over a bistro,

Which likewise caters to the flesh,
Down the street from two churches,
Where sins are forgiven, and beyond lies
St. Vincent's Hospital, where life starts and ends.

Unlike Cavafy, I harbor no desire
For boys or the cigarettes that killed him.
Unlike Cavafy, I have no "Ithaca,"
No "Waiting for the Barbarians."

A Bearded Old Poet

A bearded old poet chants his lists
of words and phrases and place-names
that make sense to him and make others yawn.

The bearded old poet dresses like a Beatnik
and lives no better in the great recession
than in the Sixties, when — fresh out of college —

he dug the middle-aged Beats — their work
he embraced like lovers — and never moved on
from the enchantment a suburban kid

felt on his first tryst with Kerouac, Corso,
and Ginsberg in the old Village haunts
they'd already put in their rearview mirrors.

The bearded old poet chants his lists,
lost in the mists of his past and the present.

Acid Peace

On the slope of Mount Wai'ale'ale
world's wettest spot
Kamalu passes out the blue caps

while we covet the last tokes
on our blunts, and rain
from Kauaian skies

tattoos the tin roof
of that folk star's warm house
well after midnight.

Swallowing the cap
I look up at the smoke
wafting to the ceiling

and nestling there
where I will soon
see the shapes of demons

and then feel the floor
collapse and let me free-fall
into the earth's core.

Sensing my panic, Malia
in purple velvet gown
begins to play her guitar

and sing heavenly songs
in no tongue, just her ethereal
voice and perfect timbre

and Puana hugs
my shoulder and says in my ear:
  We are all one, brah.

We are all in harmony
with the akua, the gods —
we are all one, brah.

And I look up into the smoke
swirling on the ceiling
and I see that the world

is good, and I hear peace
in Malia's soothing voice
and I feel safe, saved

until my flight brings me down
next day in cold gray San Francisco
and I know I have to let drugs go.

Answering the Call

Sunday morning and we are not
at the Episcopal church, where
we'd planned to go hear what
the new pastor has to say
about the Word and the world
now that she's settled in on the East
End after a decade in Concord, Waldo's
old Unitarian stomping ground,
and maybe she'd draw on her Bohemian
heritage, and I could have told her
on our way out that I'd taught two
years in Prague and speak some Czech,
but that will all have to wait
because here we are back in bed again,
worshiping at the altar of Venus,
answering the call of Priapus,
and letting pleasure, as the church bell
tolls a few blocks away, relax our
already frayed ties to the old faith.

Rats!

Where are the rats in New York poems?
Every New York poet sees a rat weekly,
But where are the rats in New York poets' poems?

When I take my garbage into the alley
Next to my building, a rat big as a cat
Waddles into the giant black rattrap:

"The rats think the traps are for shelter,"
Says my super, "when it's raining or someone
Like you messes with their territory."

Waiting for the F train at 14th & Sixth,
I watch rats scramble along the tracks,
Dining on garbage tossed there by riders,

The same riders whose hairs stand on end
And breaths cut short when a rat scurries
Along where the platform meets the wall,

Scattering folks waiting for the next train
To Brooklyn, where rats nest in Prospect Park
And pour out of brownstones under renovation,

Juicy big fat rats, prime rats, sleek as eels,
With jaws strong as a pit bull's, and tails
Wiry as water moccasins.

This is a New York poem, and it's filled
With rats in every stanza the way a New
York poem ought to be: Do you smell a rat?

Kite Flying

How much, Dad,
I used to love our forays
to the park to fly my Chinese hawk
kite in chill March winds when I'd
forget about my frayed cloth jacket
and how cold I felt as I
raced beside you, teary
eyes glommed on
to the line of twine
that ran from
your grip straight
up to the big
gray hawk
and the tail
with gaudy
orange
ribbons
trailing
behind
it
.
.
.

∽ Acknowledgments ∾

Grateful acknowledgment is made to the following publications, where some of these poems first appeared:

Blue Unicorn	"Hyacinths for My Love"
The Casserole Art & Literary Journal	"Onan"
The Deronda Review	"Kite Flying"
First Literary Review — East	"Fragment"
Five Willows Literary Review	"Acid Peace"
HitchLit Review	"Why I Never Go to Church Anymore"
Home Planet News Online	"Rats!"
Literary Matters	"Give Me Shelter (Yggdrasil's Legacy)" and "Sunday Morning"
Negative Capability	"Laura Bridgman and the Mouse"
Ol' Chanty	"Cædmon among the Cows" and "Like Cavafy"
Peacock Journal	"Desire"
Plainsongs	"A Bearded Old Poet"
String Poet	"Celestial"
Under a Warm Green Linden	"Answering the Call"
Xanadu	"Eostre / Ēostre"

About the Author

A ten-time Pushcart Prize nominee and a three-year Fulbright lecturer in Czechoslovakia, George Held taught English at Queens College for 37 years. His poems, short stories, book reviews, and translations have appeared in hundreds of publications including *Circumference, Commonweal, Confrontation,* and *Notre Dame Review,* and on Garrison Keillor's *A Writer's Almanac,* as well as in more than forty anthologies. Held's twenty-two poetry collections include *Dog Hill Poems, Bleak Splendor, Culling,* and the *Neighbors* series, animal poems for children, illustrated by Joung Un Kim. George lives in Greenwich Village with his wife, Cheryl.

A NOTE ON THE TYPE

Typography recapitulates the struggle between the *poetic* and reality. The technology that implements it must contend with surfaces that not only vary but alter the method of its presentation. Text in *Second Sight* is set in Constantia, a serif typeface doubly *transitional* — in the earliest sense of styling different (or Baroque) from the first metal Renaissance designs, and by intended use for imaging on screen in addition to the printed page.

Versatility balances simultaneous appeal to the eye of the reader and the connoisseur looking beyond legibility to the aesthetic. Designed by John Hudson, a multilingual specialist in the depiction of scripts ancient, exotic, and arcane (Ogham, Sinhalese, and Cherokee, for example), Constantia achieves benchmark fluency for continuous text, the lingua franca of contract lawyers. One of six typefaces created in conjunction with Microsoft's ClearType text-rendering technology (and the initial letter "C"), Constantia, released in 1983, takes its name from Latin, meaning "constancy." At odds with company lawyers whose fear of trademark infringement continued to narrow the choices of possible nomenclature, Hudson, one evening, singing psalms during vespers, heard "constantia" intoned. He later confessed that the sight of seabirds had made him regret that he hadn't chosen to call the typeface Cormorant.

www.ingramcontent.com/pod-product-compliance
Lightning Source LLC
Chambersburg PA
CBHW051719040426
42446CB00008B/970